COME TO THE LIGHT

COME TO THE LIGHT
An Invitation to Baptism and Confirmation

Richard N. Fragomeni, Ph.D.

CONTINUUM • NEW YORK

1999

The Continuum Publishing Company
370 Lexington Avenue,
New York, NY 10017

Copyright 1999 Richard N. Fragomeni

Printed in the United States of America

Library of Congress Cataloging-in-Publication Data

Fragomeni, Richard N.
    Come to the light: an invitation to baptism
and confirmation/ Richard N. Fragomeni.
        p. cm.
    ISBN 0-8264-1108-8 (hardcover)
    1. Baptism–Catholic Church.
    2. Catholic Church–Doctrines.
I. Title.
BX2205.F73   1999
264'.02081–dc21   99–12796
                                                              CIP

CONTENTS

Introduction

We are a sacramental church. In fact, our church is a sacrament. We are not merely a hope, we are not a good idea, we are not a party, or an agenda. We are revelation. We are an incarnation.

Those are large theological words and I'll only use a few familiar large theological words. But because we are an incarnation, we have a place, a time, a history and a recognizable body of people.

Cardinal Roger Mahoney, the Archbishop of Los Angeles, provides me with a concrete, historical document that I find inspiring. Baptism doesn't take place in a vacuum. It is happening to us in the United States at the turn of the twentieth century and when it does we have some assumptions about liturgy that shape our baptismal experience. His document, "Gather Faithfully Together," articulates some of the liturgical assumptions and liturgical contexts in which we will discuss baptism. Other ages, other contexts, would have emphasized other principles, often the principles under attack at that time or principles that would have helped a certain people in a certain place. My understanding of sacraments, especially baptism, is not handed down, it is hammered out. It is hammered out in today's church with today's preoccupations, needs and opportunities.

God takes our faith and our actions in faith seriously. They have consequences. When we are baptized, the ultimate purpose for us is the same as it was for Jesus—to be beloved children of God. When Jesus was baptized, the heavens were opened and the Spirit descended upon him and a voice proclaimed, "You are the beloved son of God." When we are baptized, it is because of our faith that a similar transformation takes place in us. So the last chapter is about the action of the Holy Spirit, the same Spirit that drove Jesus into the desert and led him through his ministry.

1

The Contemporary Liturgical Context of Baptism

On September 4, 1997, Cardinal Roger Mahoney, Archbishop of Los Angeles, published in the archdiocesan newspaper, *The Tidings,* a letter about liturgy. Entitled "Gather Faithfully Together," it was a substantial letter, with a vision of what the parish could look like in the year 2000. It projects this vision by a narrative,"What Our Lady of the Angels Parish Looks Like as the Twenty-First Century Begins."

The letter has a general introduction, a carefully articulated theology and concludes with some pastoral considerations. For my purposes, I will begin with the liturgical assumptions that should govern our church in today's world. There are five.

First, the liturgy is an act of human communication that speaks deeply the Divine Mystery. After thirty years of renewal, we see more clearly the venerable tradition that says the sacraments meet our needs, not God's. A strong theological tradition says that sacraments are for us. Because we need the sacraments to bring us into deeper communion with God and each other, we need them in a deeply human language. This human language is the language of symbols.

The word *symbol* comes from a Greek word meaning "thrown together." You sort of "catch" a symbol or your don't. You catch it with your whole person, not just mind or emotions.

This assumption that liturgy is symbolic is based on an understanding that we all communicate symbolically all the time. Even this script is a form of symbolic communication. We are wired to receive symbolic communication and we get this communication through all our sensory channels.

When we receive this, our consciousness is profoundly activated. I call this response *desire*. In the presence of sights and sounds and smells and touch and motion, we are inspired to desire, to change, to love and to know. Symbolic language awakens our desire for God.

In the presence of symbols, we begin to create visions of what reality should be. We stimulate little babies with colors, shapes and textures so they learn to know and love life. We stimulate our own if not infantile, at least immature faith life in the same way. With symbols liturgy really creates a map of the possible. It creates a map of the spiritual world. It is a multitextured, many-colored inner map, rich in sound and motion that we call a *worldview*.

You might say that with our imagination we try to make sense out of our sensory information. Our desire to know where we are and where we are going is activated. We develop an imagination and with this imagination, we reach for God. We live out of the worldview our imagination has created.

We structure a world in which what is good/bad, true/false, real/unreal, healthy/unhealthy and all our other values are located. From these value assessments, we make our decisions. From our decisions flow our behavior. Our behavior creates community and the fulfillment that comes with it. If the symbols are rich and strong, they create an alternative worldview to the consumerist society. They create a longing for another kind of life, another set of values, another map of a possible world under the influence of the Spirit. They create a longing for the Kingdom of God.

We are wired for this kind of symbolic creation. We are created for the kind of communion these symbols inform us of and call us to. Liturgy is all about the communion of saints—people with people and people with God. So the goal is not aesthetic liturgy or age-appropriate understanding of doctrine. The goal is a church that is acting out God's love for the world. The goal of the liturgy is to create a church of justice, mercy and life for the world. As stated in chapter 25 of Matthew, "Amen, amen, I say to you, whatever you have done to the least of my brothers and sisters, you have done to me."

God doesn't work magically from "out there." God works through sacramental signs. The movement of God works in a community in a sacramental system. The signs are familiar: bread, wine, oil and water but the prime symbol is the assembly of the community. That's where and through whom God speaks. Where our symbols are shoddy and our community half there, the music uninteresting and the readers mumble, God simply is not revealed and can't work. When we don't work, God doesn't work. Full, active, conscious participation is not a luxury option. It is the pulse of community life. It says that the community is alive and available to do God's work.

A second liturgical assumption is that liturgy is an action of the entire baptized community. Clerics don't do it for the people. It is not a clerical performance for the assembly. This is a life-giving symbolic exchange of the people present that activates desire and changes behavior. All baptized people have the duty of full, active, conscious participation. Musicians, readers, parents, friends, ministers—all have duties in the assembly and during the week to see that the liturgy is active and effective. Then God is present. As Regis Duffy has observed wryly, "God's real presence is always there, the problem is our real absence."

A third liturgical assumption is that God doesn't need the liturgy. We do. It is a gift. It is an aid to find peace. Ronald Grimes puts it this way: "We do what we do in the liturgy in the hope that God will do something to us. We do what we do as the assembly of the baptized, in this act of communication, in the hopes that God will do something in the middle of our doing it. We do liturgy because we need the gift God wishes to offer." Despite how crazy our church is and even crazier in our battles over liturgy itself, we need the liturgy. We should rethink our Sunday obligation. We need to be there, not to avoid offending God, but rather we need to be there for one another.

The fourth liturgical assumption reaffirms the tradition that "as we pray, so we believe." The principles of worship are the principles of faith. More than any catechism or school, we communicate our faith in the way we celebrate liturgy. The way we touch and sing and read communicates our faith—for better or worse. The liturgy activates our desire for God on a deeper level than any merely intellectual, didactic presentation can.

The fifth assumption is that the liturgy has power to transform. Not magically, but because that's what symbols do. We believe, as a Catholic community, that when we come together to receive and share, it is God speaking in these acts. The Hebrew word *dabar* means the creative word. In Genesis, God speaks and creation happens. That's *dabar.* The liturgy is God's living word, and in that living word, everything is transformed for those who are open to its power.

For the liturgy to be really human communication, it must be of the culture of the people. We call this *enculturation.* Enculturation is tricky and can go off track. Enculturation is required because we need to be able to understand and respond to the symbols. Because symbols are powerful, we use them with care. Not all language is good, even if we understand it. Not all symbols are appropriate just because we understand and respond to them. In North America, some of our cultural habits and assumptions are destructive. So our symbols can be destructive too.

Our consumerist mentality that prompts us to consider liturgy as entertainment is destructive, as is our extreme individualism and our frenetic pace. Symbols that communicate these values have no place in the liturgy. Watching television and absorbing its principles of marketing and manipulation make us feeble in our ability to celebrate liturgy or establish any communal relationships.

The liturgy practiced with these attitudes can become diabolical rather than symbolical. Symbolical means to bring together; diabolical means to tear apart. When our liturgy communicates non-welcome, bigotry, injustice, exclusivity and isolation, it is diabolical. That is also possible. Because we are always imperfect, our liturgy is always not quite a celebration of the Lord's table—yet.

Enculturation flows from the springs of the prophetic tradition. Liturgy itself must be examined in the light of the gospel. Culture must be critiqued. The church must be more than culture while being of the culture. Language is a good place to start for an example. We cannot be a welcoming inclusive community while speaking an exclusive language. We perpetuate the evils of the culture and call them holy because they are absorbed into the church's liturgy.

Theological Underpinnings

God communicates through an incarnation. In the early church, a battle arose between Catholic Christians and Gnostic Christians. Gnostics were a group of Christians who thought that Christianity saved them from this world. Body, flesh, earth, suffering and, finally, life itself were to be left behind.

The practices, especially the ascetical ones, were disciplines to get us out of our body. The body was not the temple of the Spirit, it was a prison. The soul was what mattered. What does that say about the body? The Gnostics believed the soul left this wretched body and flew way up to heaven.

Another group, Catholics, thought otherwise. More Jewish than Greek, they thought body and soul were one. They believed the body was holy, a temple in fact. The earth was sacred and the incarnation meant all parts of us were saved. The Gnostics really didn't think Jesus had a body. Bodies were loathsome, hardly fitting for the divine. Catholics said he did have a body, he did have wounds, he suffered and died with this body and we are saved by his death and the resurrection of his body. Death was merely a sleep while we wait for the body to be raised up on the last day. The Catholic side won out in theory, but in practice we still have a lot of Gnosticism in the Catholic church.

The body, the incarnation of Jesus in a body, is the central scandal of Christianity. The scandal of Christianity is that God comes to us in ordinary ways. He comes in water, in bread and wine, in oil, in touch, song and dance. Gnostics can't take that. The more the Eucharist looks ordinary, like ordinary bread, the more it is a sacrament. The more it is ordinary, the more it is extraordinary. That's scandalous. That's Catholicism. Sometimes we pretend it isn't bread. It's a "host" and we make it look unlike bread because we fear ordinary bread could never carry the presence of Christ. We want it extraordinary. In chapter 4 of Luke's Gospel, the townspeople were scandalized that Jesus was just Joseph's son—an ordinary person. They wanted something else.

There is a theological assumption that liturgy is an act of faith. We assemble because we believe. We gather as ordinary people doing ordinary things. And we know the presence of Christ in our ordinariness. We become extraordinarily ordinary. Faith is a bet; it is not the same as beliefs. A lot of people have beliefs, but little faith. Faith is a strength of the heart. We make a wager on what we cannot comprehend or see. All we see is bread and wine, water and oil, fire and song, and ordinary people. We have these parchments with the story of a man who was crucified, and we ourselves are a motley group sitting around, led by funny men wearing colorful robes and pointed hats.

We can't prove God is present. But once you've made the wager, once you've entered into the symbols and the stories, and let them shape your worldview, then the faith becomes a sure bet. Why? Because in the living together from the faith, we are nourished. The liturgy funds our faith with a richness of images so that once you live in those images a while, you begin to see in the faith they offer a peace and a profound presence within us that nothing else can give. It becomes a certitude. We have Sunday Mass week after week until we get it right. We need to get the ordinary right. We need to get the symbols and the assembly right. We need to celebrate with water and oil, sex and song, sin and forgiveness, work and play, lies and struggles within the community. We need to celebrate the ordinary. For we are Catholic. In faith, through Christ in the power of the Spirit we become elevated to be able to create a sacramental presence of God among us. So we don't do extraordinary things. We do the ordinary things well—with reverence, respect and faith. Doing the ordinary well is hard in our culture because of the cultural assumption (a lie) that we are supposed to be extraordinary.

Cardinal Mahoney, after articulating the theological underpinnings, concluded his letter to his people with some practical pastoral considerations. We need good ideas. We need to know how to put these good ideas into specific nourishing actions.

Pastoral Considerations

1. We have a deepening need for liturgical renewal. We're not there yet. We need a

lot more than just ritual renewal. Real renewal assumes spiritual and catechetical formation as well. Liturgy, spiritual direction and education all have to work together. The symbols are spoken in all those places.

2. All ministries must work together— ordained and not ordained. We need a collaborative model. The assembly must be of one spirit. A principle of subsidiarity is at work here. Subsidiarity means no higher authority usurps the work of the lower level. Many decisions have to be made on a local level. One parish is dynamic and fruitful with the assembly united in prayer and song. Another parish cannot just do what the other parish did and hope to get what they've got. Each place has its own problems and genius, and each must find faith and life according to its own spirit. All this is under the aegis of the authorities, of course, but the authorities often can't tell them how to do it. It begins with collegiality among bishops but it extends all the way from top to bottom.

3. The grand vision of the bishops must come alive at the local level. The parish, the small groups, the organizations must be fed and encouraged by the diocesan skills and resources. What do you as a

parish or group need from the larger organization to come alive in your own unique way? In a place like Los Angeles with so many cultures, the local units become quite different in experience but must be of the same spirit as the archdiocese.

4. This is more specific. We need a lot more training for people who preach homilies. Many who preach have no idea what a homily is. Liturgical preaching is different from other kinds of preaching. Before a preacher can preach liturgically, he or she needs a stronger appreciation of what the lectionary is. We do not read the Bible at the liturgy, we read the lectionary. The lectionary is the church's interpretation of the Bible. (Biblical scholars gag at the cut and paste found in the lectionary!) We read Luke in the third year of the lectionary cycle, we read his parables long after Easter when Christ is dead and risen. That's not the sequence or the plot in Luke. A homily also requires communication skills, not just sincerity. The liturgy is living communication. If the preacher is dead, then that's what goes into the microphones and that's what infects the assembly.

5. Liturgy finds its fulfillment as the source and summit of Christian life in worship.

Worship is not the same as liturgy. Liturgy is the sacramental symbolic activity of a community in which it receives and yields to the gift of God. It does so by thanks and praise. Worship is how much all that liturgy is worth to us. The true worship of the church is the activity of social justice and life in the world. The prophets say that the true worship of God is feeding the hungry, taking care of the widow and orphan. The liturgy shapes a church that acts on God's love for the world. The goal of liturgy is Matthew 25 already quoted; "Amen, amen, I say to you, whatever you have done to the least of my brothers and sisters, you have done to me." We render God praise by pouring out our lives in service and compassion for the world. We renew the liturgy in order to renew the face of the earth. The gift we receive in the liturgy isn't complete until we in turn give it away. That's the worship of God.

Baptism: Going Back to the Water, Coming into the Light

I invite you to meditate on a profound mystery. Sometimes we can forget this mystery. It is the paschal mystery of the one who serves us and who is with us and dips us and enables us to die in order to transform us in shape and color and form and spirit.

Perhaps you could meditate on this by understanding this mystery in "grandmother time," a time to do nothing but bask in the vacancy of our hearts so that God in mysterious ways might speak. Our theme in this will be "Going back to the water, coming into the light." I will try to help you renew and reexamine the role and significance of baptism for us.

Allow me to go back as far as we can in the documents of the church to find what our ancestors spoke of when they spoke of baptism. Let's go to the year A.D. 100. Our locale is a small northern African town where Tertullian lived before he became a heretic. He wrote a document to defend his position against adversaries who suggested that baptism was to no avail. His document was in Latin. Its title, *De Baptismo.* In it he suggests that baptism is indeed efficacious because baptism is a drowning in the water. He says baptism is efficacious because God always uses simple things.

There were some Gnostic heretics at this time who asserted that baptism in simple water could not avail anything. How could anything as simple as water do anything as magnificent as was claimed in baptism? We claim that new life is given, that the church is reborn, people are regenerated. Tertullian was defending the most orthodox of Catholic teachings. It is in the simple, elemental things that God speaks in the most extraordinary ways.

When we go back to this early treatise, we notice that three-fourths of it is engaged in the praise of water. Water is praised at the beginning of creation. It is praised from the side of Christ, in the River Jordan, in the Red Sea, in the river that flowed through the city of God in the eternal Jerusalem. Tertullian praises water as that ordinary, simple element that pagans praised and that pagans used. But now in Christ it has become the plunging place. It has become the place to make the plunge into God.

He is quite clear that the word *baptism*, as you may know, means to drown to death. To be baptized means to be held under the water so that one experiences what fish experience—learning to breathe in a new way.

Let me share three points from his baptismal treatise. The first is that the ordinary reveals the extraordinary. That's the fundamental Catholic principle. We believe that ordinary things reveal the extraordinary power of God. Leonardo Boff has a wonderful little book, *The Life of the Sacraments, the Sacraments of Life.* He talks about a cigarette that his father smoked on his deathbed. Leonardo wasn't able to be at his father's death and when he arrived his father had already died.

But there on his bed stand was a little cigarette butt his father had smoked before he died. His mother had saved the little stub and now in his little book, Leonardo has saved it as well. He has it on a special little box on his desk. That small cigarette becomes the ordinary experience of something extraordinary—the presence of his father.

He sees in that cigarette butt something that opens up. He says it opens up into something transparent. It elicits a transcendent experience of his father. He calls this the sacramental principle of Roman Catholicism. Somehow, ordinary things open up to extraordinary presence. The immanent becomes transparent to something transcendent.

As Catholics, we do this all the time. We see in ordinary bread and wine something that opens up into something transparent, so that something transcendent appears. Think about it in view of your own experience. A friend of mine recently died and left me his shaver. He left me this shaver because he was always amazed that I could get such a smooth shave. I told him it was because I changed blades every once in a while. So when he died suddenly in a car crash, I inherited his shaver. It is now on my desk just as Boff's father's cigarette butt is on his. Somehow that shaver becomes transparent and my friend Steve appears as a living presence. Perhaps you've had similar experiences. Leonardo Boff, in talking about sacraments, says that is a wholly ordinary human experience. This symbol becomes transparent and that's exactly what Tertullian describes when he describes water. Water is ordinary. It is efficacious because with the eyes of faith and love, the water becomes transparent. It is the means of a divine washing. The divine Spirit washes and cleanses, heals and restores us to a community of believers. This is the Catholic thing. We believe ordinary things become extraordinary. We do so because of faith.

You all remember the old Latin song "*Tantum Ergo?*" *Tantum ergo sacramentum, veneremur cernui. Et antiqum documentum, novo cedat ritui. Praestet fides supplementum, sensuum defectui. Praestet fides supplementum sensuum defectui.* It should be translated: "Let faith supply where the senses are inadequate or defective. In the eyes of faith, ordinary things become transparent to something extraordinary." It all depends on the eyes of faith. So when we enter into the baptismal water, we enter with faith. This water becomes something regenerative for us. It must be entered into with faith. What is faith? Faith is surrender. It is yielding ourselves to what we cannot see. It is trusting what we do not know. It is putting ourselves on the line. It is the risk of entering into that which cannot be understood or known through our senses. It is entering into the ambiguity of the water.

Tertullian also suggests that entering the water is risky business because it demands that we die. It demands that we surrender everything. So not only do we believe the water becomes transparent to some divine power, we believe it also means that entering into the water means that everything has to be left behind.

Perhaps a personal story will bring this home. A few years ago I had the opportunity to do some bodysurfing. Did you ever bodysurf? I was in Hawaii and I had never done it before. It is an act of tremendous faith. Three of my friends came with me when I went to Hawaii to teach. I was working while they were vacationing. But I did have one afternoon off, so they invited me to come with them to the ocean. I'm not a great swimmer. I probably passed "minnow" at the "Y" as a kid. I went anyway. I didn't even have a bathing suit.

They told me not to worry. Boxer shorts would be sufficient. So I wore them. "Now you can do some bodysurfing," they assured me. "The way you do it is just watch for a big wave, run directly into the wave and then you see what happens." I said OK. I had a sort of primitive faith. I made my wager. I ran into this large wave. But I tried to hold on because I panicked. I tried to manage the wave, but it just took me. In a few seconds I realized there was no way of controlling that wave. I had to surrender myself in that wave. The wave turned me over and over—it seemed to be forever. Finally, it threw me back on the shore—but without my underwear!

Tertullian is talking about baptism as that kind of yielding to the water. Because in order to allow ourselves to be baptized in the water that is the revelation point of some divine power, we must surrender into it. Up and down and over and around. It takes a long time to surrender into that water.

If you are of a certain age, you probably remember from the catechism that we said that baptism gave us a character. It described that character as an indelible mark on our soul. That was the old way of talking about character. Three sacraments created character: baptism, confirmation and holy orders. Edward Schillebeeckx in his wonderful book, *Christ the Sacrament of the Encounter with God,* redefines character as a dynamic relationship rather than a static mark. For instance, in holy orders the character is a new and unique relationship with the community as presbyters, deacons and bishops. Think about the character of baptism as a relationship with water—a permanent relationship with water. Once we are plunged into baptism, we are in a new relationship with water. We must continually surrender into the water. There is no letting go of the surrender that has to take place. That water can turn us over and around and can reveal to us something of the divine Spirit that we would otherwise not know.

What Tertullian is after is the awareness that to be baptized means that we are always being baptized. We live in a baptismal mode. None of us has surrendered enough into the water. When that surrender happens—in the water—we are stripped naked. We leave our old mode of life behind.

I don't know about you. I usually have one foot in the water and one foot on firm land, and if my clothes come off I want to put them on again—quickly. Including gloves and hat. In brief, I want to be in control.

To be baptized means we are not in control of the water. The water is in control. The water, which is the divine experience, the immanent place where the transcendent is made transparent, now holds us, owns us. We must serve the water. It is the power of God into which we are baptized. We must yield to the blood of Christ.

We are in the midst of an inner dynamic that says we must keep on dying. We yield, bit by bit. We are to live in one sense under the water. That's the character of baptism. If we leave the water we do not live at all, which is the third image Tertullian brings to us.

Tertullian is combating a Gnostic heresy, as I mentioned, which held that simple, ordinary things cannot do extraordinary things. He insists on the Catholic tradition that ordinary things surely do yield powerful results. He holds that, if you enter into the transforming water, something enormously powerful can happen in faith to those who have eyes and who are constantly being overthrown in that water. He uses a great image. He says we have to be like little fish. Little fish following the big kahuna! The Greek word for fish is *ichthus,* a title we often give Christ. He plays off that word because it is an acrostic. In Greek, the first letters of the words "Jesus Christ the Son of God and Savior" spell out the Greek word *Ichthus.* Tertullian says that if you really want to be baptized, you have to see yourselves as little fish and you have to be able to breathe under the water.

We need to learn to surrender and learn to breathe under water. What does it mean to breathe under water? If you were to breathe under water, what would you do? Drown. In other words, if we want to follow Christ, the big fish, learn to drown. Not just surrender a little, that means to let the water take care of you, but this is a step deeper, it is allowing the water to drown us. To kill us. To breathe under water means to breathe death. It means to live an alternative way of life. It is a new mode of surviving, breathing water instead of air. Now death is the mode of survival. Drown! This is the baptismal imperative.

I remember I was in Lourdes a few years ago. You can take a bath in the Lourdes water. It is an experience not to be forgotten. You walk into this big room. There are two pools—one for men and the other for women. (In the early church they baptized the women first and then the men. They were baptized naked.) So you undress. They wrap you in this sheet and you wait your turn. You go in and they hold you down in the water! For a moment I thought I was drowning. In the early church, that was the experience. Some of you may have baptismal pools in your churches yet.

We got away from this drowning experience in baptism and we made it sanitary. We do that a lot with our sacraments. We pretend they are not really sacraments. We don't let their power speak. Baptism is an ordinary drowning event. In Lourdes, I was drowning, fighting to come up! Three times they plunged me underneath the water and three times I had to fight—unsuccessfully for a long time—for air. Then a miraculous thing happened. I got out of the water and I wasn't wet! There was something there that made me dry off immediately. I don't know how to fit that into my schema or my rational understanding.

Tertullian is clear, though. To be a baptismal person, one must learn to be like little fish and learn to breathe under water. We follow the big fish, Jesus, who was crucified and breathed life into death and turned death into life. If we wish to be baptized, we must learn to live in that paradox.

What does that ultimately mean? It means that there must come within us a dispossession of the self. The extraordinary experience of dying must become the ordinary experience of living. The baptismal character recognizes that the dispossession of the self in love, in association with Christ—that plunging into the sea—is who we are. We are to keep on drowning, keep on dying. That is the message of baptism and the foundational experience of Christian life.

I don't know about you, but I want to live. I don't want to surrender. I don't even want to see the ordinary be extraordinary. I want the extraordinary to be extraordinary. Like everyone else in America, I live in a culture that is thrilled by the extraordinary. I want to be like the early apostles, who wanted Jesus to come down off the cross. Like Peter, I don't want him to wash feet. I don't want him to be born in Bethlehem, or to come from Nazareth. I want something extraordinary. But the Catholic tradition holds that the extraordinary is embedded in the ordinary; in ordinary events like coming from Nazareth, being born in a little town called Bethlehem and washing feet. We Catholics believe in stuff such as bread and wine and fire and oil. I want something extraordinary. But Tertullian reminds us, and baptism reminds us, that it is ordinary water.

I don't know about you, but I don't want to surrender. I want control. I want to tell the associate pastor what to do. I'm the boss. Don't argue with me. How dare they tell me after eight years of seminary training and eight years of graduate school, what to do and what to think. I don't want to surrender in relationships either. I don't want to say, "I'm sorry, I was wrong." I want to look like I'm right and like I've got it all together. I don't often want to breathe death either. I don't even want to face the fact that my hair is falling out, much less mortality. I don't want to look at people who are suffering sometimes, because it is too painful to face the fact that I'm going to go six feet under. Sometimes I can get really hard and cold at a funeral. I don't want to think about my own. That's what baptism keeps asking us to do! Surrender. Surrender in love.

But I get glimpses through the water of what it might be like to live in the freedom of breathing underneath it. Just glimpses. The glimpse is this: I am a new creation and I am free. There is no more fear and no more guilt or shame, because I am no longer I who live, but gradually in glimpses, when I am at my best, I begin to see in that surrender, in that dying and in that ordinary water that it is Christ who lives in me.

We don't want our sacraments to be ordinary. Even when we celebrate Eucharist today, we have bread that doesn't look like bread. We pretend it isn't ordinary! We are scandalized by the ordinary. So we make it look like it is extra-ordinary rather than being ordinary bread that crumbles and breaks. And in baptism we use silver bowls and elaborate fountains rather than the pools and streams used long ago. We are scandalized at the fact that things so extraordinary can come in such ordinary things. In the ordinary, the extraordinary appears. It all comes in the surrender that we make in faith, the willingness we have to believe death, the death of Christ.

Let me conclude with St. Paul:

> For surely you know that when we were baptized into union with Christ Jesus, we were baptized into union with his death. By our baptism, then, we were buried with him and shared his death in order that just as Christ was raised from death by the glorious power of the Father, so also we might live a new life. For since we have become one with him in dying as he did, in the same way we shall be one with him by being raised to life as he was. We know that our old being has been put to death with Christ on the cross in order that the power of the sinful self might be destroyed so that we should no longer be slaves of sin. For when a person dies, he is said to be free from the power of sin. Since we have died in Christ, we believe that we shall also live with him. For we know that Christ has been raised from the dead so that he will never die

again. Death will no longer rule over him. So because he died, sin has no power over him and now he lives his life in fellowship with God. In the same way, you are to think of yourselves as dead so far as sin is concerned, but living in union with God through Christ. (Rom. 6:3–11)

I want this to be a little more than just information. I'm going to give you a few questions to help you integrate your baptism into your life. I hope you'll find them nourishing for you personally.

1. What part of you still refuses to be plunged into the sea of baptism?
2. What part of you refuses to die?
3. What part of you can be yielded and surrendered so the water may overtake you?
4. What causes you to want to jump out of the water and put on your shoes and socks?
5. What part of you does not want to breathe under the water?
6. When will you be totally baptized and die?
7. What bit of you needs to die?

2

Baptism as Illumination

$\mathcal{T}$he sacrament of baptism has traditionally been called an illumination. It is clear why baptism might be a dying, even a dying into rising. But the relationship to light is a little more complex and has to do with the nature of faith. When we plunge into the sea of baptism in order that we might see, what is it we do see when we have vision? Understanding baptism as a sacrament of death and rising introduces us to the mystery of baptism as a mystery of faith. We understand faith as a type of seeing, a mystery of light, of enlightenment, the way of light as opposed to the way of darkness. We need to explore that movement from darkness to light a little more.

In the *Didake,* a first-century document, the author suggests that for those who are preparing for baptism, two ways lie ahead: the way of light and the way of darkness. John Paul II uses that same metaphor in his *Evangelium Vitae* where he talks about the culture of death and the culture of life. The earlier tradition was the culture of light and the culture of darkness. Baptism, as a sacrament of dying with Christ, introduces us into the way of light.

The way of light is always associated with the power of the Holy Spirit. Jesus entered into the way of light at his own baptism when the Spirit came upon him and led him into the desert where he was presented with choices between darkness and light. The Spirit sent him with vision to combat the powers of darkness in the desert so that his own ministry could be clarified. In the temptations, he saw more clearly what it is that brings us light and what brings us darkness. The Spirit opened his eyes so that he could clearly see the way of God.

Think about the temptations of Jesus. The first one was to change stones into bread. Jesus says, quoting Deuteronomy 8:3, "People do not live by bread alone but by every word that comes from God's mouth." The second one was to "jump off the parapet of the temple and let the angels catch you." But Jesus said, "You shall not put the Lord, your God, to the test." In the third temptation, Satan leads him to the highest mountain and says, "All these kingdoms of the world I will give you if you will bow down before me." Jesus responds, "Worship the Lord your God alone."

The way of darkness and the way of light are always the two paths. Baptism illumines us in the

Holy Spirit so that we might choose the way of light. What were Jesus' temptations about? The answer, to me, is simple. They were about short-cuts. Jesus was about feeding the poor and showing people the true way of power. He was about reordering human society. The devil was saying, "Look, I will give you all the shortcuts you need. Change these stones into bread and by magic you will feed the poor. Jump off the parapet, let the angels catch you, they'll think you're a super-hero and then they'll all come after you, and you'll be able to do what you need to do. Bow down in front of me and I'll make you stronger than any politician, and you'll be able to change the government and economic and religious systems." The devil was offering him a shortcut to his ministry.

In all three, he refuses. He refuses the way of darkness because now, in the Holy Spirit, he sees that it is only in conversion of hearts that the poor will be fed. Only by conversion of hearts, not by transformation of stones, will the poor be fed. Only in weakness and brokenness will strength occur, not in jumping off buildings so angels will catch you. Only in service and humility, not in political or economic reform, will it all happen. That is the way of light. It is in the way of conversion, of weakness, of poverty, service and humility, that we are baptized.

We all, in one way or another, have such temptations. We all have, if you will, the opportunity to choose between light and darkness. Baptism has illumined us in the same Holy Spirit so we can see clearly with Jesus. We can discern the way of light over darkness. To see clearly is always the miracle Jesus performs when he opens the eyes of the blind. When he opens people's sight, he gives them the Spirit to see clearly and be able to live in the light.

We see clearly in four ways. The first is that, in order to see clearly in the light, we need to be aware of the machinations of human consciousness. Consciousness itself is often distorted and lives in darkness. We are all conscious. It is a fire within us. It allows us to perceive and to see, to hear with clarity. We see because we are conscious. It is a gift of God. But it has a second layer. We can become conscious that we are conscious. (Try it. For a moment, just be aware that you are aware.) Not only do we perceive with our senses and consciousness, we're also able to step back and become clear about knowing that we know. We know when we know.

The ability to be aware that we are aware, conscious that we are conscious, is the gift that is clarified in the sacraments. We are always conscious that we are conscious through a specific lens. That lens can be one of darkness or light.

Baptism and the whole Christian experience of death and rising in Christ leads us to a third level: we can become critically conscious that we

Baptism as Illumination

are conscious. This is complex. That is why people go to spiritual direction. That's why we go to psychologists. That's why we meditate and write in our journals. We want to become critically aware of how we are aware of our awareness.

We've learned that the lenses we strap on can be clouded in darkness. Critical conscious consciousness allows us the freedom of baptism and illumination. It allows us to be aware that our consciousness lenses are biased. I am aware that the way I am aware is flawed. That's called *critical conscious consciousness*. In biblical terms, I am aware that I am a person born blind. I am born a person who doesn't see. But what is worse is when, like the Pharisees in John's Gospel, I am not aware that I don't see. Jesus reserves his criticism for them. He condemns them because they say that they see and they really don't (John 9:41). They are not aware of their lenses. They lack critical consciousness. It is not accidental that biblical scholars consider chapter 8 of John to be a baptismal preparation text for the early church.

It is to the freedom of that consciousness that the baptismal illumination is addressed. The darkness of critical conscious consciousness is bias. For example, I never realized I was racist until I moved to Chicago. I grew up in a racist community and didn't know it. We were taught,

by my parents' actions and the actions of neigh-
bors, not to like either people of different color
or different nationalities. That was just part of my
lens. That's how I was consciously conscious. I
was looking through a racist lens. I was simply
not aware. I never noticed what I was doing looking through that lens until I taught students of a
different color. I realized I didn't like them! I realized I disliked them not for something they were
doing, but because of something within me that
wasn't enlightened yet. Part of me was not critically conscious. It took therapy and some spiritual direction to make me critically self-aware. I
became free only when I became aware of my
bias. I still have a racist capacity but I'm critically
conscious of it. When any racist tendency
appears, I can understand it is a childhood lens
through which I need no longer look.

This critical consciousness illuminates us as
the gift of the Holy Spirit given in baptism. We can
authentically live in our little worlds, but our hori-
zon is terribly inauthentic. For example, I never
realized that, for me, being a Roman Catholic
meant that I had all the answers. I assumed no one
could offer me anything. My childhood lens was
that Catholicism was the whole truth and nothing
but the truth.

When I started talking to my Buddhist,
Jewish, Hindu or Muslim friends, I thought I was
always above them. I believed they had no truth to

Baptism as Illumination

give me. Equipped with all the answers, I simply tolerated them. There was no real dialogue until I began to listen to them and realized they were making a contribution to the conversation I could not make. This forced me to step back from my lens and become critically conscious of my assumptions. I began to see how my lens was dark and distorting. I thought darkness was light. That's the biggest deception of darkness. Darkness convinces you it is light. I had to step back and accept the grace to see I don't have all the answers and my friends have a lot to teach me.

When I was first ordained, I acquired the lens of "Father, you're in charge." I was 25 years old, I had a copy of *The Documents of Vatican II* in one hand, the *People's Mass Book* in the other and I virtually said to the people, "You're going to love this. You're going to sing what I sing and think what I think. I'm a priest and you're not." One day a lady remarked, "Father, when are you going to get off your damned high horse and be like the rest of us?" She knocked my lens off. I realized my view through this lens was not that of an enlightened spirit. Gradually I dismounted and took off my lens of clericalism. That too was of the devil, of darkness.

All consciousness is filtered through lenses. The lens most prevalent in the church today is sexism. Some people just don't "get it." Not getting it is our way of saying that someone has a lens of which they are not conscious. "Seeing, they do not see" (Matt. 13 : 13) was the way Jesus put it. Until we become critically conscious, we are not free. Our baptismal enlightenment is not really activated yet.

We can also become historically-critically consciously conscious. Simply put, we can see the origins of our biases. In the enlightenment of the Spirit, we can step back far enough to see where our biases originated and we no longer have to be stuck in them, like the blind leading the blind. I think the Second Vatican Council was such a moment of enlightenment. It was illumination for the church. After 400 years of bias against Protestants, we began to take off that lens. With historical illumination, we learned the origin of our hatred for Protestants. We learned they were baptized; they were not going to Hell, as Father had taught us. We had an elaborate dark lens, the origins of which we were not critically aware.

Gradually, some of us became suspicious of that lens because we had Protestant friends. Now we are gaining friends from every tradition. We go back to the roots of our bias and we realize that anti-Protestant sentiment is of darkness.

As baptism frees us from our sin, it enlightens our vision. Baptism is freedom from blindness, even when that blindness is all around us. Bernard Lonergan suggests that we all have blind spots. In the old theology, we said merely that baptism freed us from original sin, the original blindness that keeps us from perceiving God in our hearts. We can become critically conscious of the ways in which we block God. We become historically conscious of the ways that as a nation, a culture, and a church we have blocked God. The amazing grace is that blindness has been freed in baptism and we no longer have to live in the darkness.

Even the old Baltimore Catechism said that, while we have been freed from original sin, the original blindness, the effects of it, are still around. There is still blindness, dimmed consciousness and bias in mind and heart as we refuse to live in the Spirit. We clutch our limits and refuse critical consciousness. We love our darkness. We do not want increased consciousness. It's as though the light hurts our eyes.

We come to celebrate that we have been reborn and no longer have to live in the darkness. St. Paul puts it this way to the Ephesians:

> You yourselves used to be in the darkness but since you have become the Lord's people, you are in the light. So you must live like people who belong to the light, for it is the light that brings a rich harvest of every kind of goodness, righteousness and truth. Learn what pleases the Lord. Have nothing to do with the worthless things that people do—things that belong to the darkness. Instead, bring them out to the light. . . .

For anything that is clearly revealed becomes light. That is why it is said, "Wake up, sleeper, and rise from death and Christ will shine on you." So be careful how you live. Don't live like ignorant people. (Eph. 5:8–15)

Here let me paraphrase: "We are uncritically conscious of the biases and lenses by which we operate in our parishes, the power plays that happen and the hatred we have for people we've never met simply because they may look like someone we disliked long ago. This is why I think that we who are ministers and leaders must engage in spiritual direction and counseling. We have so many unexamined biases we inculcate in our people unconsciously. We are in leadership positions. We are called not to be ignorant of our own limits. Unless our own consciousness is critical, we cannot proclaim light and freedom. We don't even see the darkness of racism, sexism, ageism, consumerism—all the lenses of darkness. They can all be caught up in Christ. Paul has told us, not to live like ignorant people but like raised people. Make good use of every opportunity you have because these are evil days. Don't be fools then, but try to find out what the Lord wants you to do. Live in God's light.

When Jesus was baptized, his consciousness in the Holy Spirit was illumined. He could see the tricks of the devil, the traps in the easy way out. He saw through the lures of magical tricks and shortcuts. He wouldn't play the politico-religious institutional game. Instead of playing the tricks inherent in the bias of darkness, his open heart allowed him full consciousness of the way of God. The way of God is always the way of conversion of heart: weakness, poverty, service, humility and love. These are the ways of God. I believe that the more we are baptized and begin to enter into the water and begin to see, the more our conscious consciousness is purified and illumined, and the more aware we become of our own darkness. Then we are truly people of the light. Then the light will shine through us and then there will be no more darkness.

We live in darkness because our consciousness is blind. We cling to our blindness when we refuse to let the Spirit wash us again in the illuminating waters of baptism.

I invite you to meditate on these personal questions:

1. Are you aware of the assumptions that lead you to understand what you understand?
2. Are you willing to let those lenses of assumptions be purified by the Spirit?
3. Are you willing to let the Spirit reveal your secret blind spots to you?
4. Do you know your personal symptoms of blindness—your triggers?

3

Baptism: Our
Vowed Response

$\mathcal{L}$et me summarize what we have explored so
far. We have an eternal character with water. We
return repeatedly to that ordinary water that becomes transparent. We find ourselves drawn into
the water. We are lured into surrender in those
waves that upend us and lay us bare. We find ourselves plunged into the death of Christ. As fish
breathing under the water, our self-surrender in
death is a self-surrender to love. In this sea, we see.

We see like Christ with the power of the
Holy Spirit who illuminates our minds and consciousness. We see the way of darkness and we
are invited into the mystery of light. We are enlightened so that we will no longer be ignorant.
We are made critically conscious in illumination
so that we might be like Christ. As such, we must
see clearly the distortions of darkness. We become aware of the original sin of our tendency to
exclusion, our love of shortcuts and our need to

control through force and power rather than by humility and meekness.

In the waters of baptism, we begin to see with increased consciousness the cycles of human affairs, the cycles of evil to which we have been born and are a part. We see the isolation and the insidious sin of this world. Racism, sexism, nationalism and consumerism are dark lenses through which we customarily see from birth.

Baptism frees us so that we might become illumined, enabled to see the darkness and to enter into the mystery of light. It is for this we have been plunged into the water. We are to see as Christ sees. This is how we put on Christ and enter the way of Christ. We do this all in the water.

Now let's move on to our part in this journey from death to life. How do we claim this death by volunteering to continue it? We die with Christ in the water by making vows. We put on Christ by claiming his death as ours by a vow. We make vows to Christ who first vowed to us. He vowed an abiding presence. He first vowed to us a perpetual relationship—God with us, Immanuel. Our vow is in response to his.

The image of the vow of baptism again comes from Tertullian. The word for vow in Latin is *sacramentum*. Tertullian took this notion of vow or *sacramentum* from the Roman soldiers.

You can almost picture Tertullian hiding behind bushes watching soldiers as they go through boot camp, which he identified with the catechumenate of his time. He would actually watch the soldiers in the boot camp. As the training was completed, Caesar would gather them all together and ask them to take an oath, a *sacramentum*. "Vow to me, in good times and bad, in sickness and in health, your allegiance." They would respond, "Caesar, we will be loyal soldiers to you even to death for you. We will go to war for you . . . etc." Once they made this oath, they were branded as soldiers of Caesar and there was no way out. Except death. The vow was for life. Tertullian borrowed the term and concept from Roman military practice when he was examining what Christians were doing in the waters of death and enlightenment.

May I suggest we distinguish between a vow and a contract? The terms *vow* and *contract* are business terms. This is true in marriage and priesthood also. A contract is something you enter knowing the terms. You know what you're getting into. The contract must be clear, neat and clean on the paper. You can hire a lawyer to make sure you know what you're getting involved in. Business deals work better when you read the fine print. You don't want any surprises. If you don't read the fine print, you're not too bright.

Currently, many marriages are becoming contracts instead of vows by the device of the prenuptial agreement. There is a way out and they know ahead of time what that way is. (A question for canonists would be whether a prenuptial agreement is an impediment to covenanting a Catholic sacramental marriage. It puts a restriction on the arrangement, changing the vow to a contract.)

An oath or vow or covenant is made without any idea of what you are getting yourself into. But you do it anyway. That's the "better or worse" part of the marriage vows. A vow is an unconditional plunging into the water. You enter without restriction because of the love you wish to express in taking that oath. Many enter marriage or priesthood as a contract, not as a covenant. We'll stay as long as it is fulfilling for us. We'll stay as long as I'll get something out of it for me. The expectation turns the vow into a contract. But a vow is without condition or expectation. (I think we make a grave mistake in equating a civil and valid marriage with a sacramental marriage. They are two separate realities. Most people enter marriage as a contract and gradually begin to enter it as a covenant. How else do you explain the large numbers of divorces and our attempts to get around them by what we call *annulments*. I think this has gotten out of control. We annul anything with a head. What does this say about the sacredness of the vow of marriage?)

We now baptize adults, often without the necessary scrutinies and evaluations, if they want to be baptized. We still indiscriminately baptize children. It seems to me that until we take baptism as seriously as we do holy orders, we haven't really understood the phenomenon of being Christian and Catholics. We take holy orders more seriously than we take baptism. But the vows of baptism are more essential than any other vow.

I think the problem with the disruption of the vows of marriage and holy orders is because we haven't taken the vows of baptism seriously.

Now the question becomes, Why do we dare take such oaths? Why do we make such a *sacramentum?* Why do we take such oaths in the water? My only answer to you is, because Christ first took the oath to us. We do it in imitation of God who is faithful to us and who has entered into covenant with us unconditionally. God, making no reservations, entered into a covenant with humanity and continues to be loyal to that covenant. When we are disloyal, God continues to be loyal. In view of that immense love, and in view of the power of that covenant, we dare stand in the water of death and illumination and make such vows.

We use ritual words. "Do you reject sin, so as to live in the freedom of God's children?" And we say, "I do." "Do you refuse to be mastered by sin?" "I do." "Do you believe in God, the Father almighty, creator of Heaven and Earth?" "I do believe." And in Jesus and the Holy Spirit and the Church and the Resurrection? We answer, "I do." We repeat the vows. And we renew these vows in the unrelenting covenant and oath God has made to us in perpetuity even to the end of time. We make these ritual words in the water as an oath.

The problem is that these are ritual words. At some point in our Catholic career, in our vocation as disciples, we have to stop and ask ourselves in a critically conscious way, What do those words mean? When we say we will reject sin and live in the freedom of God, what do we understand? When we say we believe, what do these words mean?

I think they mean this. They mean that, in response to the great oath that Christ has made to us, we vow to be Christ. We vow to be the body of Christ. We vow to surrender ourselves and our own identities to a Christlikeness. We vow to surrender our own darkness and our own unredeemed consciousness to a Christ-consciousness. We vow to be Christ, and like Christ, to make an unconditional commitment of availability to God and one another. I simply believe that the oath of baptism is this: we vow in Christlikeness to be available to all creatures and all creation. We vow to be Christ for all people in their need and in their pain and to be available, inclusively, to all. We vow to be of service to all for the freedom of all from the bias and bondage of sin. We vow this Christlikeness. It is to that vow that we are committed under the water. For life. We are under that water. We keep breathing under that water until we get it right.

Our vow declares it is no longer we who live, but Christ who lives within us. He lives through our consciousness, through our dying, through our critical awareness. He leads us beyond our addiction and sin. We vow to lay down our lives so that Christ will breathe in us.

In other words, the vow of baptism is an oath that we make because Christlikeness demands that we become Christlike in the small things—to the person, for instance, whom we are most irritated by. Marriage, friendship and ministry all demand that we surrender ourselves and lay down our lives for each other. We do this without questioning, without justifying our behavior or attitude. The oath of baptism does not put us first. It puts Christ first. The oath allows Christ to take us over and in the Spirit to become the living sacrifice of praise to God. That's why being under the water is a lifetime commitment.

In the old days, this vow character was called a *habit*. As a habit, certain acts are so ingrained they become who we really are. That's why we are always being plunged under the water. The Spirit keeps inviting us to critical consciousness. That's why we keep on celebrating the Eucharist repeatedly. It must become our habit. We must become indistinguishable in our oath from the oath that is Christ's oath. We demonstrate with our inclusivity and service and freedom from bondage that our vows of baptism make us the body of Christ.

St. Paul has the final word. In his letter to the Philippians (2:1–13), he writes:

> Your life in Christ makes you strong and his love comforts you. You have fellowship with the Spirit and you have kindness and compassion to one another. I urge you, then, to make me completely happy by having the same thoughts, sharing the same love and being one in soul and mind. Don't do anything from selfish ambition or from a cheap desire to boast but be humble toward one another, always considering others better than yourselves. Look out for one another and one another's interests, not just your own. The attitude you should have is the one that Christ Jesus had. He always had the nature of God, but he did not think that by force he should try to become equal to God. Instead, of his own free will, he gave up all he had [in a *sacramentum*] and took the nature of a servant, and became human and appeared in human likeness. He was humble and walked the path of obedience all the way to death, death on a cross. For this reason, God raised him to the highest place above and gave him the name that is greater than

any other name. And so in honor of the name of Jesus, all beings in heaven and on earth and in the world below will fall on their knees and all will openly proclaim that Jesus Christ is Lord to the Glory of God the Father. So dear friends, as you always obeyed me when I was with you, it is even more important that you obey me now that I am away from you. Keep on working with fear and trembling to complete your salvation because God is always at work in you to make you willing and able to obey this oath that you have taken.

I recommend you meditate on this question. How deeply am I immersed in the vows of baptism?

4

Baptism:
The Anointing

$\mathcal{T}$he oath or vow of our baptism is the *sacramentum* that unites us. As we commit ourselves more and more deeply to this oath, we as church become the *sacramentum,* the living vow, the living image and the living presence of God. We become the body of Christ. In that vow, our Christlikeness shines forth. Women and men in the vow of baptism are plunged and the ordinary—that's us—becomes extraordinary.

We become transparent. We reveal the presence of the living Christ when we are church. In the vow we are plunged into the surrender of self-sacrificing love. In the vow, we are caught up into the breathing of water which is the death of Christ. In the vowing, we are made available to others in their need forever. That is how Christ made himself available to us in our need forever.

I remember when I was a kid, we were asked the question by the Sisters: "Why did God make you?" We would dutifully answer, "God made me to know him, to love him and to serve him in this world and to be happy with him forever in heaven." Recently, some spiritual writers have suggested that that is a B+ answer. It is the right answer, but it is the wrong question. The right question to that answer would be, "Why did Christ plunge himself into our humanity?" "Why did Christ take the oath of his baptism?" "Why was Christ baptized in the River Jordan?" "Why was he baptized in the blood of his own cross and pain?" The reason we are able to love God and serve God above all things is that God in Christ, and in Christ's baptism, first came to know us and to love us and to serve us in this world so that we might know everlasting life.

So in our vowing, we make ourselves available to those in need forever, as Christ was available to us in our need. We are caught up by a divine invitation. We are invited to imitate the divine. We can now more closely understand why *divinization* is what our Greek and Russian Orthodox brothers and sisters call baptism. Our baptism is for the forgiveness of sins. We are forgiven so we might live in light and be enlightened. And in a clarifying of consciousness, which we have called an historically-critically conscious consciousness, we might see as Christ sees.

As Christ, we begin to operate in the liberating activity of the prophet. (I will develop that more fully in the last chapter.) We are Christened in baptism. Baptism makes us another Christ, first, before any ordination ever could. It is in Christ that men and women become the other Christ.

The ritual of baptism moves us from the water to the oil. In Christ, in the water, in the coming into light, in the vowing that we make, in this Christened nature we share in baptism, we are anointed into the one who is the anointed one.

What does it mean then, to accept the messianic anointing, emerging from the water, wet with the vows, to die and live and breathe under the water? What does it mean to live a life totally guided by the Holy Spirit? What is it to invoke the higher power and thus, in our baptisms, to become creatures and children of the light. We become creatures of God, creatures of the light—the Pentecost light, the firelight, the wind light as in tongues of flame. What does it mean to be anointed in the Spirit as Christ? I invite you to meditate on two passages in the New Testament. The first is chapter 8 of Romans:

> Now there is no condemnation for those who live in Christ Jesus. For the law of the Spirit which brings us life in union with Christ Jesus has set me free. Free from the law of sin and death. What the law could not do because human nature was weak, God has done in the water and

the Spirit. He condemned sin in human nature by sending his own Son who came with a nature like our sinful nature; to do away with sin. God did this so the righteous demands of the law might be fully satisfied in us who live according to the Spirit and not according to human nature. Those who live as their human nature tells them to do have their minds controlled by what human nature wants. Those who live as the Spirit tells them to have their minds controlled by what the Spirit wants.

Thus the anointing with the oil in what we now call *confirmation*, the messianic anointing in Christ, is what illuminates the lens of our critical consciousness so we see through the eyes of Christ, the pneumatic Christ. We no longer see through the eyes of our human nature. Paul uses the Greek term for "flesh" where I used "human nature." The problem with calling our human nature "flesh" is that in our time and culture, we assume the body is bad. The notion that the body is bad is a heresy, specifically Jansenism. To be controlled by human nature results in death. To be controlled by the Spirit results in life and peace. A person becomes an enemy of God when controlled by human nature. He does not obey God's law and, in fact, he cannot obey it. Those who obey their human nature cannot please God. *"But you do not live as your human nature tells you to, you live as the Spirit tells you to, if, in fact, God's Spirit lives in you. Whoever does not have the Spirit of Christ does not belong to him."*

If Christ lives in you and your human nature has died underneath the water, and if you have been freed from your human nature, then the divine nature that God gives us in the Spirit is life for us. We have been put right with God, even though our bodies are going to die because of sin.

If the Spirit of God who raised Jesus from the dead lives in you, then he who gave life to Christ will also give life to our mortal bodies by the presence of the Spirit in us.

We have an obligation not to live as our sinful human nature wants to live. If we live only according to our human nature, we are going to die. But if, by the Spirit, we put to death our sinful actions, we will live. Those who are led by God's Spirit are God's children. The Spirit that God has given us does not make us slaves and cause us to be afraid. Instead, the Spirit makes us God's children and by God's Spirit, power has been given to us. So we cry out, "Abba, Father, my Father." God's Spirit joins our spirit to declare that we are God's children, children of light and messianically anointed. We are made the family of God in the water like little fish. Since we are his children, we will possess the blessings he keeps for his people. We will possess with Christ what God has kept for him. For if you share Christ's suffering, we will also share his glory. Paul continues:

> For I am certain that nothing can separate us from his love: neither death nor life, neither angels nor heavenly rulers or power, nor the present nor the future, neither the world above nor the world below. There is nothing in creation that will ever be able to separate us from the love of God which is ours through Jesus Christ and through the power of the Spirit which has anointed us.

To be anointed in the Spirit is to be separated from our human nature. The great philosopher Bernard Lonergan calls *sarx,* or human nature, spontaneous introversion. There is something out of whack with human nature. It spontaneously turns in on itself in anger, hate, blame, greed and lust. It turns in on itself to protect itself, for survival. When I was driving up here yesterday my spontaneous introversion showed up. (I'm not drowned or anointed yet, either.) When I'm driving, wearing a roman collar, I don't make certain gestures at other drivers. But when that jerk cut me off, and then made an obscene gesture, I came within a hair of exposing certain fingers to him, too. Probably the only reason I didn't was because I was wearing the collar. There is something in us that is spontaneously turned in ourselves. In baptism that is the human nature we are asked to die to. To be in the habit of the vow we take, we are to find a new spontaneity in the Holy Spirit. The fifth chapter of Paul's letter to the Galatians spells out a bit what this new spontaneity looks like. *"What I say to you is this: let the Spirit with which you are anointed direct your lives, so that you might be anointed as Christ was anointed."* You will not satisfy the desires of human nature. What our human nature wants is opposed to what the Spirit wants—quite spontaneously. These two are enemies and that means that you cannot do what you want to do.

If the Spirit leads you, then you are not subject to the law. What human nature does is quite plain, Paul says. *"It shows itself in immoral, filthy and indecent actions, in worship of idols and witchcraft. People become enemies and fight. They become jealous, angry and ambitious. They separate into parties and groups, they are envious, they get drunk, have orgies and do other things like this. I warn you, those who do these things will not possess the kingdom of God."* If you notice, those things of spontaneous introversion are not all about sex.

The Spirit produces love. If we become spontaneous in the Spirit, it turns into love, joy, peace, patience, kindness, goodness, faithfulness, humility and self-control. There is no law against these things. Those who belong to Jesus and have been baptized into Jesus have put to death their human nature and its spontaneous introversion with all its passions and desires. The Spirit has given us life and must also control our lives. We must not be proud or irate with one another, or be jealous.

Once we are anointed with the oil through the water, the Spirit erupts spontaneously within us like a fountain. Then we know the true meaning of the word *spirituality*. We hear a lot about spirituality today. Add it to anything and people come to the workshop. The word *spirituality* is simple in its origin. Tertullian originated the word *spiritualitas*. It means simply life in the Spirit. There is only one Christian spirituality, one Catholic spirituality. There is only one spirituality because there is only one Spirit and only life in the Spirit, and we have been anointed in that Spirit in the oil of baptism and confirmation. In that Spirit we have been Christened and we live. That is, baptismal life is life in the Holy Spirit.

We have been baptized into the anointed life of the Holy Spirit. As the Spirit descended upon Jesus, it descended upon us.

5

Baptismal Spirituality

$\mathcal{L}$ ife in the Holy Spirit is our "spirituality." In the past twenty years, there has been a lot of talk about spirituality and some confusion as to what the word means. So I've divided spirituality into four categories.

Once we have the "habit" of the baptismal Spirit, growing in the water, plunging more deeply, what is this thing called spirituality? The first understanding of spirituality is simply life in the Holy Spirit. It's life given totally over to Christ and the Holy Spirit in response to the Spirit given to the church in baptism and confirmation. It is a life no longer lived in the degenerate spontaneous introversion of human nature. It is now life yielded to the Spirit from above, the descending Spirit that transforms us. In this sense there is only one Christian spirituality because there is only one Spirit. One Lord, one faith, one church, one body—the body of Christ.

There is another meaning. In order to live in the Spirit, we must continue the death in the water, which is difficult. We're always being torn away. We are led astray from within and without. So holy people throughout Christian history have invented disciplines to help keep us in the one Spirit. They are modes of engaging this baptismal habit. Francis, Dominic and Benedict each invented one. We have the rosary, Lourdes, relics, processions—we have all forms of piety that have been invented to move us more deeply into the one spirituality. All these forms are good but they are optional. Some of them are sentimental (pitying Jesus as the prisoner in the little white host just isn't helpful) and have to be quietly dropped. On the other hand, genuflecting before the Blessed Sacrament is salutary, it is a bending of our ego that helps us.

In the past, some of these disciplines substituted for the original spirituality they were to serve. They became fluff, veneer, sentimental, and got in the way of the life in the Spirit. Life in the Spirit has to have the characteristics we read about in chapter 5 of Galatians. Piety without those may be enjoyable, but it is a distraction. They can even become diabolic, as people use them as religious tools to clobber people over the head. They become sort of religious passive-aggressive acts of violence.

Nevertheless, these disciplines are very important. They were created, like training wheels, as a support for our baptismal plunge. Sometimes we can take disciplines from other traditions. For instance, Thomas Keating has written a book on centering prayer. This prayer came from the Hindu tradition of meditation and Keating learned it as a form of transcendental meditation. Anthony de Mello also baptized a lot of Hindu techniques very effectively. Teresa of Ávila and John of the Cross invented such disciplines as well. Their effectiveness is in their repetition. They open us to deeper life in the Spirit. The only official discipline in the church is the liturgy.

There is a third meaning of the word spirituality. It refers to the growth and development of the human spirit. Many secular writings refer to spirituality and they simply mean fuller human development. They don't mean life in the Holy Spirit which transforms the human spirit, they just mean full human potential. We see this in scientology, for instance or the human potential movement. The goal is simply full realization of our human potential.

There is a fourth meaning and it, like the third meaning, refers to those disciplines which enable you to fulfill your potential. Psychotherapy would fall into this category, as would the enneagram or the Myers-Briggs personality inventory.

These secular spiritual disciplines and full human development are extremely important, because grace builds on nature. You have to know who you are in order to surrender who you are. These disciplines are necessary to secure the human spirit, so it can be broken open at the feet of God.

The waters of baptism go beyond human development. They require we surrender our human potential in order to be transformed into the Spirit of Christ. John Donne describes this in his sonnet XIV:

> Batter my heart, three-personed God, for You
> As yet but knock, breathe, shine,
>   and seek to mend;
> That I may rise and stand, o'erthrow me, and bend
> Your force, to break, blow, burn,
>   and make me new.
> I, like an usurped town, to another due,
> Labor to admit You, but Oh, to no end!
> Reason, Your viceroy in me, me should defend,
> But is captive, and proves weak or untrue.
> Yet dearly I love You, and would be loved fain,
> But am bethroned unto Your enemy:
> Divorce me, untie or break that knot again,
> Take me to You, imprison me, for I,
> Except You enthrall me, never shall be free,
> Nor ever chaste, except You ravish me.

The human heart can get all pumped up with secular spirituality. We have all these techniques in contemporary culture. We call them spirituality, like the spirituality of being a better businessman, priest, golfer or basketball player. You get someone like Tony Robbins with his infomercials. He pumps up people so they realize their full potential. We live in a world in which we are supposed to strengthen our ego and build up ourselves. But Donne is right. If we have entered into the water, then we must pray, *"Batter our hearts, O God. Break these egos that we worked so hard to build up. For unless you enthrall me, I shall never be free. I will never be chaste except you ravish me."*

The spiritual disciplines of our tradition serve to put us in harm's way, to allow ourselves to be ravished in the water. So be careful of what disciplines you do.

Unless the disciplines of our tradition have a living awareness of the role of the Holy Spirit, they degenerate into the last category of disciplines that merely strengthen the human spirit, like therapy or Myers–Briggs. What was originally designed to enable us to surrender can be used quite subtly just to build the ego. Jesus knows about that. Two people went up to the Temple to pray. One was a monsignor; the other was a woman who had just had an abortion. The monsignor was doing all the disciplines of our tradition but he was doing them merely to strengthen his ego. The woman who had just had an abortion, beating her breast, said, "O God have mercy on me, a sinner." She goes home justified. Spiritual disciplines can degenerate into merely human disciplines. Watch it.

The proof that our disciplines (retreats, rosary, office, processions, visits to the Blessed Sacrament) are effective rests on how clearly they support the first category: life in the Spirit. The proof is that we live in charity, in mercy, walk humbly with our God and do justice.

The official way that our baptism is deepened is the discipline of the Eucharist, especially the Sunday Eucharist. (Daily mass is quite different from Sunday. People go to daily mass usually to pray for a deceased loved one or they want to go to communion.)

Life in the Spirit, under the water, takes discipline. It is the habit of the vow. It takes years and we need other disciplines to help us be disciplined in the spontaneity of the Spirit. Those other disciplines have been called spiritualities by the church.

There is only one life in the Holy Spirit. Christian spirituality is life in the Holy Spirit. This is the spirituality we read about in Galatians 5 and Romans 8. These have developed through the years and assist us in surrendering more deeply to our baptismal plunge. Sometimes these disciplines can even get away from true life in the Spirit if they become ends in themselves.

They can be twisted a bit just to help us find our own human spirit.

I have no problem with various human disciplines to help us find our best human spirit but the point is that in baptism we are called to surrender our human nature to allow it to be transformed by the life-giving Spirit.

So the term *spirituality* is often used in three ways. First, it is life in the Holy Spirit. Secondly, it refers to the various disciplines that lead us into life in the Spirit. And, thirdly, it is life in our own human spirit. For the Christian, the one true spirituality is life in the power of the Spirit given to us in baptism.

6

Baptismal Values

When we are anointed and illumined by the Spirit then everything begins to be seen in a different light and our values change. We develop the values of a prophetic consciousness.

The disciplines of prayer and liturgy, of the religious orders and our various acts of piety readjust our values. Here are some of the values that enable us to breathe under water.

We value human touch so necessary for our survival. You've read the stories about babies who died because they weren't touched. The value of human touch in the Spirit becomes the holy kiss, the kiss of peace. We cherish nonviolent communion with one another rather than inflict sexual and physical abuse. In the Spirit, human touch and bodily presence get caught up in the presence of Christ. Christ is incarnate in us. In touching one another, we know the presence of the Spirit. Physical abuse is at an end.

Our self-centered egotism becomes dispossessed in love in the Spirit. We surrender to one another. I am no longer the center of my existence. Christ is. My human enterprise has Christ as central to my growth. Bernard Tyrell has written a number of books on Christotherapy. If you want your ego to grow, then you must find that the ego is regenerated only in Christ. We must decrease, he must increase so that Christ becomes our new center. I think egotism is particularly harmful in those of us who are leaders in the church. Have we really put Christ at the center of our lives? Or is our ego still in control?

Our lives can stagnate, even in religion. We stagnate when we think we've been reborn and that's it. I've read the Bible and I've studied theology: I've arrived. I think the Spirit moves us into a new value, the value of continuing conversion. Continuing transformation is based on the realization that the more we know, the more we know most of our knowledge is false. We realize we are free to unlearn in order to learn anew. We realize that stagnation of mind and heart can become deceptive. "I've got all the answers, thank you."

Another value is the recognition of denial in our culture. We deny death, sickness, poverty and aging among other things. But in the Spirit of Christ, we can embrace human change. We can embrace human suffering and dying. In embracing it, we find ourselves liberated. We like to forget things. We don't want to remember. "That was in the past. Forget it." We do that rather than remember human suffering and human victims and in the memory of that pain continue our struggle for human liberation. After all, we celebrate a hanging! In the Eucharist, we celebrate a capital punishment. In remembering the death of Christ, we remember all victims. In the Spirit we recognize we are part of a larger cosmos.

This self-centeredness of ours, thinking that we are here to subdue the earth, yields to a recognition that in subduing the earth, we only pollute it. We wreck it as we use it only for our human interests. In the Spirit, we recognize we are part of a larger creation. Our relationship to the things of the earth and the whole cosmos is an intrinsic part of being baptized. No Christian should pollute.

In the Spirit we see that the mechanics of the institution of the church are only secondary to the persons who are the church. In the Spirit we move away from institutional values. The church as an "it" or a "they," or merely a structure, gives way to the church as a community of persons. We are reconciled to be free from division, jealousy and the survival of the fittest.

In the Spirit we come to recognize that as Christians we are baptized not to save our own anatomies. I remember once we asked our nun, "Why did you become a nun?" She replied, "Because I am afraid of maternity." In the second grade, we all wondered what maternity was. She was from Italy and we didn't understand her English, so when I went home and told my mother that, she called the sister. Of course, she was afraid of "eternity." In the Spirit we let go of being a priest "to save my soul," or being a Christian because "I am afraid of Hell." If those are our motives, we can call that imperfect contrition. It gets you there, but it limps badly.

We recognize that the value of being a Christian is not to save ourselves; the value is in being called, not because we are great but because we are the scum of the earth! We have been called by Christ to give witness to the New Age. We are called to give witness to the power of the Spirit in a degenerate world. We have been chosen in our weakness to be ambassadors of reconciliation. Sister was wrong. We are Christians because we have already been given the gift of eternal life now. We are called to proclaim that gospel of mercy forever.

Again, I offer some questions to help you assimilate this understanding personally:

1. Whom in your life have you forgotten? Or would like to?
2. Whom do you love least? We are only as close to God as we are to the person we love least.
3. How close to God am I? I am as close to God as I am to my community, however I define it.

7

Baptism and Eucharist

$\mathcal{L}$et's examine the Sunday celebration as a baptismal renewal in the Spirit. I suggest the Eucharist does this in four ways.

The first is the discipline of community. We cannot live in the Spirit unless we live in community. Nobody is saved alone. That's a Protestant, especially American Protestant, understanding. Our tradition says there is no salvation apart from a community of faith. We pushed that over the edge when we used to say that if you weren't Catholic, you couldn't go to heaven! But the intuition that we are saved in community is sound. We understand that salvation comes in relationships.

The second discipline is one of narrative or story. To live in the Spirit, we must embrace the biblical story. During the last thirty years, the Catholic community has retrieved that discipline through scripture study, sharing and private reading. We had to overcome a traditional fear of "private interpretation" that prevented us from reading the scriptures. We did read Bible stories that were interpreted for us. Our homilies were not homilies. We read the scriptures, put them aside and preached on a topic that usually came from a manual. For example, we would have sermons on forbidden movies and then we'd have to get up and take the pledge. But now scripture study and reading is much more strongly encouraged. We memorized catechism, not scripture.

Most of us grew up not in a biblical narrative, but in a medieval narrative. In the 1950s, our view of reality came from Dante, not Isaiah, Moses and Jesus. Now we more clearly understand that this life is God's dwelling place. God is in the affairs of human history, in the struggle for justice, and we see Christ crucified in the victims of this world. If we don't find God's presence now, we never will. This universe is not a sinful place but is charged with the grandeur of God. In the medieval narrative of the 1950s God was an ogre, watching to catch me in sin. In the biblical narrative, God is a housewife who sweeps the kitchen until she finds the lost coin.

The third discipline is one of giving thanks and praise. To live in the Spirit, we give thanks and praise and there is a difference between the two. Thanksgiving is the opening of our hearts to receive the gift. To be disciplined in gratitude is to observe the discipline of letting oneself be overwhelmed by a gift. In the Eucharist, we come to allow ourselves to be ravished by the gift of the Spirit, given under the water. To give thanks is to give nothing to the one who is giving. If you try to reciprocate, you insult the giver.

Praise, on the other hand, is a different disposition. Praise is standing in awe of the beauty of the one who gives the gift. Together, praise and thanks are a discipline. This needs to be translated into the week's activities. We say that we give thanks and praise always and everywhere. How do we give thanks and praise on the highway when someone cuts us off? Or attacks us? How do I give thanks for the gift of their attack and then give praise? How do I stand in awe of the beauty of the ugly attack? That's a serious discipline.

The final discipline is one of eating and drinking. It's the discipline of being a human being with a body. We relish our incarnation. We honor the plan that says we must eat and drink to survive. We recognize that God comes to us in our humanity, not to save us from our humanity. We honor each other's bodies and the body of Christ. As we saw, an early heresy called Gnosticism said that the body was a prison. It is not a prison for us, not in our Catholic tradition. For us it is the arena of revelation. The Eucharist is a discipline that teaches us we are humans in need of food and drink. As St. Augustine said, "In the food and drink that we receive, we become part of the Eucharist, so our bodies are transformed into the living flesh and blood of Jesus."

The celebration of the Eucharist is the height of Christian initiation. It is the ultimate Christian discipline. It combines the discipline of community, narrative, thanks and praise and the acknowledgment of our incarnation in eating and drinking. In those disciplines, we plunge more deeply into the water.

8

Baptized into
the Believing
Community

Certain images sum up our return to the baptismal water. The first is from Maya Angelou in her book *Wouldn't Take Nothing for My Journey Now.* On pages 73-74, she describes her earliest memories of her grandmother whom she called mama.

> It is a glimpse of a tall cinnamon-colored woman with deep soft voice standing thousands of feet up in the air on nothing visible. That incredible vision was a result of what my imagination would do each time mama drew herself up to her full six feet, clasped her hands behind her back, looked up into a distant sky and said, "I will step out on the word of God. I will step out on the word of God." . . . The depression, which was a difficult time for everyone, especially for a single black

woman in the South, tending her crippled son and her two grandchildren, caused her to make her statement of Faith often. She would look up, as though she could will herself into the heavens and tell her family in particular and the world in general, "I will step out on the word of God. I will step out on the word of God." Immediately, I could see her flung into space, moons at her feet and stars at her head, comets swirling around her. Naturally, since mama stood out on the word of God and mama was over six feet tall, it wasn't difficult for me to have faith. I grew up knowing the word of God has power.

We've been discussing how, as we enter the baptismal water, we also recognize, no doubt, that we are stepping out on the word of God that has been passed on to us as faith from our ancestors. None of us could step out on the word of God unless faith was a gift. Faith is a gift of God, but it doesn't come from God directly. The faith we enter in baptism is a gift of our ancestors. Where did you receive your faith? The plunge into baptismal faith comes to us from the local church and is passed on. Ultimately it is a gift from God but you have to go back sixty-one generations to the apostles.

They got this risk of a faith, with all its uncertainty, from Jesus. Our faith is a gift from Christ from the Father. He has been with us sixty-one generations. We stand out on the word of God because our ancestors did. We stand out on the power that comes from Jesus. From his baptism, he stepped out on the word of God to begin a ministry that would change history.

At his deciding moment, setting his face toward Jerusalem, Jesus stepped out on the word of God. He did it in Gethsemane, where he wrestled with the word of God: to go forward to his exodus or not.

As he uttered words of forgiveness, as he hung dying he, stepped out on the word of God. We are witnesses to all of these things. We witness that the word of God has never failed. No matter how much doubt, no matter how much suffering and violence, it has not failed. We are witnesses to his new way, the way that comes from the baptismal water of enlightenment. We are witnesses to a way that leads to true reconciliation and peace. This is the way of forgiving love when the victim of violence steps out on the word of God. It has proved more powerful than any force or violence, even death itself. This way leads to resurrection.

The second image comes from a short woman. I was preparing for a talk to an upper-class suburban parish. I was making the Way of the Cross when a little old lady came in, about four feet tall and dressed like a cowboy. (I learned later she was a psychiatrist.) She came up to me and said, "You the priest?" "Yes." "Are you the one who's going to talk to us?" I affirmed. She said, "What are you going to talk about?" I said, "Music and liturgy." She said, "Is it going to be any good?" I smiled and said, "Lady, I'm going to do the best I can." She said, "Father, to do the best you can— that's what saints are made of."

In the character of baptism, we have become the saints of God. With our relationship to the water, the oil and the Spirit, we have become the saints of God and we are called to do the very best we can. We proclaim the vow of baptism in what we say and what we do. We are called to be loyal and faithful, and available to others in their need forever. That is what saints are made of. We do the best we can to stand out on the word of God.

The third image is from a poet, Denise Levertov. Her poem is entitled "The Beginning of Wisdom," and she's quoting Proverbs 9:10:

> You have brought me so far.
> I know so much: names, verbs, images, my mind overflows.
> A drawer that can't close.
> Unscathed among the tortured, ignorant, parchment uninscribed, light strokes only where a scribe tried out a pen.

I am so small, a speck of dust, moving across the huge world, the world a speck of dust in the universe.

Are you holding the universe? You hold on to my smallness. How do you grasp it?

How does it not slip away? I know so little. You have brought me so far.

I've thrown out a lot of images. We've come so far. We know so much. We might say, with Thomas Aquinas, we've known so much, we've thought so much—and yet we know so little. We've been brought so far. We've come so far that even when we know we've done the very best we can, we know so little. We know so little of this mystery that surrounds us. The mystery is infinitely comprehensible. It is the mystery of water and oil and Spirit, bread and wine, community, word and narrative, thanks and praise. Besides the mysteries of God and world, there is the mystery of our own humanity. We acknowledge we know so little and then we claim God has brought us so far.

Sometimes we think we know so much and have so much certainty. But have we really stood out on the word of God that calls us into darkness, even a dark night of the soul? It is a darkness one faces under water. When we stand out in faith, we acknowledge we know so little. In that uncertainty, we repeat the vows of baptism.

As Jesus said, "Why have you forsaken me?" and then, "Father, into your hands, I commend my spirit."

You are familiar with Nike's slogan: just do it. When we live under the water, when we stand on the word of God and live in the Spirit of God, then the Holy Spirit changes everything. Just do it becomes, under the reversing power of the Spirit, "Do it just." Do it justly. Don't just do it. Do it compassionately, mercifully, the best you can. Just doing it becomes perfunctory and routine. Ask any married couple. If they just do it, it becomes boring. What we do, we have to do with our whole heart and soul.

My last image comes from an educational journal. Common advice, from knowledgeable horse traders, includes the adage, "If the horse you're riding dies, get off." This sounds like simple advice. But we don't follow that in our lives, our ministries or our churches. Instead, we choose alternatives such as trying a stronger whip, switching bridles or riders. "This is the horse we've always ridden." Appoint a committee to study the dead horse. My favorite is, "Arrange to visit other sites where they ride dead horses more efficiently." Hire better riders. Compare how we ride now with how we did it twenty years ago. Complain about the quality of horses and even blame the horses' parents.

That's why we jump into the water—to get off the dead horse. We go under to get out of the darkness, sin and neuroses. We are willing to dismount when we learn we can ride the eagle's wings.

9

Life in the Baptismal Spirit

$\mathcal{A}$fter discussing some deeper understandings of baptism for the person baptized, let's turn now to some of the social consequences of baptism. We have seen that baptism gives us a new life in the Spirit and Paul clarified some of the personal changes in our lives that Spirit would bring about

But in our tradition, the Spirit is not only the author of moral and spiritual clarity within the individual, She is also the source of moral and spiritual sensitivity for the community. The Spirit not only whispers in our private ear the truth we must live, She also speaks more publicly about the moral and spiritual life of the community. If we are to be saved in community, we must live in a community that is saved. The community is saved by listening to the prophets. That's one of the reasons Jesus chastises the Pharisees, accusing them of killing the prophets (Luke 11:47). When they did, they not only committed individual murder, they stilled the life force of God's chosen people.

When She speaks as the conscience of the community, we call that prophecy. In our tradition, we have narratives of the Spirit speaking. Let us meditate on five places where the Spirit speaks prophetically: the Hebrew prophets, Jesus, the apostles, the church and the poor.

She breathes and blows where She wills. Her message is consistent. The message is "renew the face of the earth." She creates and dislodges, builds and tears down, comforts and destroys, gives and takes life. The Holy Spirit is the baptismal gift of the Father and the Son that blows freshly and freely. She inspires hope beyond despair and beyond any institution we create or idea we realize. She is the one who creates and re-creates the face of the earth. There is no stopping the power of the Holy Spirit.

We must be an in-spired, in-spirited people. We often feel the opposite, we feel dis-spirited and even in despair because of what we face on our streets, homes and neighborhoods. My prayer is that my words can, in some small way, communicate through narrative and story to in-spirit (or inspire) you. Otherwise we both waste our time. Only the Holy Spirit can renew the face of the earth. Together we will conspire. Together we can breathe the same Spirit.

Cardinal Mahoney said in his letter to his archdiocese, which we mentioned at the beginning of this work, "The goal of all liturgy is to renew the face of the earth. So when we receive the Sacrament of the Eucharist, we become agents of God's power and love and justice in the world." May we conspire toward that goal. It is tragic when there is dissension and wrangling about liturgy, when the goal is to find the common ground in the Holy Spirit.

Not to push the linguistic argument too far, it is fair to say that, when we find this common ground and are motivated by the Holy Spirit, we will work hard for the Kingdom. We will "per-spire" in God's service, we will sweat in our ministries! Then we are the glory of God, fully alive, manifesting the Spirit within us. Then all we do and all we say will be inspired by the Holy Spirit within us. Then whatever we do is done with Christ, in Christ unto the glory of God the Father who breathes the Spirit into us, calling us into the prophetic role.

The Holy Spirit brings the virtue of hope. Hope is not the same as hopes. We can have a lot of hopes and yet not much hope. When our fondest hopes are dashed, we still have hope. We have hope as long as we are open to the Spirit. Hope is being open to the surprise that God always works and God's ways are not our ways, that God is re-creating the face of the Earth. God re-creates in the divine image and likeness, not ours. So we celebrate the Spirit that opens us to the surprising action of God.

The Holy Spirit speaks the prophetic word through the prophets. They were a motley group. They were too young to speak or too old or too sinful or too mealymouthed (like Isaiah) to receive the gift of the Spirit. Yet in their words and in their actions they appeared at decisive moments in Israel's history, when Israel had gone wrong, forgetting that God's ways are not our ways. When Israel worshipped falsely, the prophets appeared. They spoke in hope of a new creation as the established institutions broke down. They spoke of destruction and alternatives in the Spirit. The prophets pointed to the new possibility of God breaking through with justice in covenant promise.

The best example I can offer is the remarkable ways in which the prophets counteracted the sacrificial laws of Israel (see Isa. 58:1–9 for a fine example). Israel became too caught up in sacrificial laws. (This sheep or that one? This shape of altar or that one? What kind of knife?) They had institutionalized sacrifice without meaning. The prophets preached and made a breakthrough. They said, "God doesn't want all that stinking bloody beef burning on his altars!" (The priests kept the best part of the beef, of course.)

The prophets decried this in the Spirit and they declared boldly their critique of that which blocked the working of God and the communion of the people. The priests had become so careful of the rubrics of sacrifice they had forgotten the meaning of sacrifice. The prophets said, "God doesn't want your holocausts, your incense, your fatted calves."

They spoke clearly. What does God want, then? "Feed the hungry, take care of the widow and the orphan. Give your bread to the poor and for God's sakes, don't turn your back on your own kind." When the prophets spoke thus in the Holy Spirit, they spoke prophetically and they inverted the social order, for which, of course, they were stoned. The penalty for dislodging the institutional meaning of sacrifice is death. You all know that. It is always dangerous to speak prophetically. We still celebrate this in a song you all know. "Come, Lord Jesus. Send us your Spirit. Renew the face of the Earth."

The Holy Spirit speaks prophetically in Jesus of Nazareth. When you look at the Gospel of Mark, our earliest account, you see that the Holy Spirit speaks over Jesus at his baptism. At that moment, Jesus opens up a whole new understanding of baptism. Jesus speaks in the Spirit not only for the remission of sins, as was John's baptism. When the Spirit spoke over Jesus, Jesus was now to baptize with both water and the Spirit, not only for the remission of sins but also to preach the reign of God. Jesus' work, ministry and miracles were not only for the forgiveness of sins. Jesus, led by the Spirit, comes back and breaks open John's baptism by adding a new dimension. He now preaches something beyond forgiveness of sin: he preaches that the reign of God is in our midst.

The gift of God's terrible mercy is in our midst, the outpouring of love. God's mercy is more than forgiveness, because in the power of the Spirit, Jesus even overturns what forgiveness means. On the fourth Sunday of Lent (Cycle C) we read the gospel of the Prodigal *Father*. In that story Jesus reverses John's baptism, because John's baptism is only for the forgiveness of sin. Jesus announces that when sins are forgiven, those forgiven sinners receive bounteous gifts that they do not even deserve! That's what so outraged the elder son in the story. He could tolerate his brother's sins being forgiven, but what he cannot accept is the celebration of the gifts the wayward one receives. The Father goes overboard. The elder son cannot handle and will not condone this prodigality. Such is the surprise of the Spirit. Jesus proclaims that the Father showers gifts on people who don't deserve any gifts.

That's why we don't believe in capital punishment. We do not believe sinners should die for their sins. We believe in boundless grace for the guilty—for all of us guilty ones. We believe, and celebrate sacramentally, that sins are forgiven and the sinner is given the richness that only God can give. That's what the prophet Jesus taught.

We believe that even someone who doesn't deserve to live deserves to live in the overwhelming mercy of God. It is acutely incongruous that we can go out and picket for "right to life" (which we should) and then turn around and scream to take the life of a sinner. God's ways are not our ways. When Jesus speaks prophetically in the Holy Spirit, he goes beyond the baptism of John.

Like the prophets before him, he reverses the Sabbath law. He speaks to women. He embraces strangers. He welcomes outcasts, sinners and lepers. His Spirit sought and still seeks to dislodge and subvert the oppressiveness of established powers. His Spirit still surprises us with new ways that are not our ways. He was crucified for it like the prophets before him. The powers are always threatened by the movement of the Holy Spirit. She's a dangerous bird!

The Holy Spirit speaks prophetically through the apostles. This was another motley crew— a group of fishermen. They disappointed Jesus frequently, especially at his most desperate hour. We celebrate the apostles in the Pentecost victory. On Pentecost, the gift of the Spirit blew in on them and their fear was reversed into boldness. They went out and spoke languages everyone could understand. People thought they were drunk with spirits (our word and theirs for booze) but they were only filled with the Spirit. Would that we would be so drunk, so bold, so overflowing with enthusiasm.

The most interesting moment where the Spirit was speaking through the apostles was when they had the battle about the question of circumcision. It was an institutional law at the time that Gentiles wanting to be Christians had to be circumcised as Jews first. "Salvation comes through the Jews," was the saying that governed them. The belief was that one had to be a Jew first, then you could become Christian.

The debate took sides between the institutional church in Jerusalem and the prophetic spirit in Paul. The Acts of the Apostles records the first ecumenical council in which they battled over the question: "Do men have to be circumcised as Jews before they can become Christian?" The institutional church, with a little prompting from the Spirit, changed its mind and the law was changed.

A question for us: If the institutional church decided that this male ritual was not necessary, does that say something about who can enter the church? Was this not a preoccupation with male membership, whether they admitted this or not? If males were the only ones who could be circumcised, and that was a precondition for entry, wasn't that a preoccupation with the only ones who really mattered? Is this a clue about the openness of the early church to the role of women?

I wouldn't put it past the Holy Spirit. Doesn't it say also, in one breath in Galatians, "There is no more Jew or Greek, no more male or female, slave or free person?" When it gets translated a few years later, the phrase "male or female" disappears. It is up to you to decide in which of those cases the Holy Spirit is prophetically active.

The Holy Spirit speaks prophetically in another place, the lineage of the apostles. In a document called the *Teaching of the Apostles* (*Didaskalia Apostolorum*) the bishops are told, "If you are celebrating midnight mass in your lavish cathedral and you are sitting on your throne and you see a poor person enter in the back, get off your throne, give the poor person that seat and you, if you have to, sit on the floor." What would happen if a poor woman in rags sat on the throne at the cathedral in one of our major cities? The answer is clear, vivid and largely unacceptable: the Spirit would be speaking. And it sure would disrupt the face of the earth! Those are the kinds of things the Spirit does when She speaks through the apostles. The structure and order of the community are inverted.

The Holy Spirit speaks prophetically in the charismatic community. By baptism, the Holy Spirit has been unleashed and we have been renewed in water and oil. Now all baptized are beginning to rediscover what the Holy Spirit has made of us. Our Holy Father has written that the first and primary symbol of the liturgy is not the priest but the assembly of believers, which includes all the ministers. It is the body enlivened by the Spirit, the charismatic community, that symbolizes the presence of Christ. That is the place in which the Spirit continues to speak prophetically.

Many of us grew up in a church dominated by clerics. I grew up thinking the Holy Spirit could only speak through Father or Sister, not through the community. Those days are usually safely behind us and we know differently. The reality is that I am a priest; you and I are together called to enliven the community that gives voice to that Holy Spirit. We are all called to a variety of ministries that will build up the community. Then the community will renew the face of the earth. Together we build the kingdom of God on earth and together we work for what we pray, "Thy kingdom come." We all have different ministries, but what we really bring to the community is our common humanity. Perhaps we should consider our navel as revelatory! It is a fine sign of our shared humanity. That's what we share. It is our renewed and baptized humanity that constitutes this prophetic community.

Every charism, every sacrament, every individual renews the community. This understanding can reverse the clericalism that I grew up in, and that some are trying to restore today. The emergence of the gifts of the laity is not superfluous, is not a luxury option. These gifts are not decoration or a favor handed out by Father. They are the structure and substance of the building of the body of Christ for the transformation of the world. Perhaps the declining number of clergy will highlight the work of the Spirit active in the entire community. As communities continue to catechize and preach the word, bishops will need to face a new ordering of the church—a prophetic ordering.

The Holy Spirit continues to speak through the martyrs who continue to die for the gospel even in parts of the world that haven't seen a priest for years. Could it be that the Spirit is whispering a new way of being church? (I know I'm on dangerous ground here.) How will the charismatic community be ordered in the charism of the apostles and the apostolic tradition when there are fewer and fewer presbyters to order it?

Perhaps the bishops are opening themselves to the recognition that the celebration of liturgy must continue. The catechesis must happen. The gospel must be preached. The Holy Spirit is still working even though She may be working in the whisper of a new way of being a communion.

Finally, the Holy Spirit speaks prophetically in the mouths of the poor who are marginalized and oppressed. There is a difference. The marginalized poor are those who are pushed out as outsiders. They don't belong. The oppressed poor are inside the system, but inside they are oppressed economically and racially, among other ways. It is from the edges that we expect to hear prophetic voices. The mouths of the poor speak the real agency of God.

The reality of poverty is great and in the process of struggling for liberation these persons stand up in courage and righteousness: the Spirit is speaking. The voice of the Spirit calls the systems and structures to a renewal so that all are welcomed. None is marginalized. When we have created those systems of power, we can re-create them in the power of the Spirit. Johannes Metz declares that the mouths of the poor speak prophetically when they become the subjects of their own lives.

In the work of the hands of the poor, they remind us and lead us back to the earth. The earth itself and all creation have been oppressed. The earth has been oppressed by pollution, its inhabitants oppressed by hate. We look to the poor in the women's community, in the liberation community, in the advocacy community for the old and the unborn. We see the prophetic edge in their oppression. They are stoned. The Spirit speaks best from the poor because She speaks from the underside of power, where you least expect Her voice.

I've suggested five ways the Spirit speaks prophetically. In all five areas, She speaks the subversive good news of God's reign in God's will and God's ways which are not our ways.

Let me leave you with a few questions to consider:

1. How do we, as a church, test the truth that it is the Spirit speaking and not the evil spirits? Three criteria: (1) Inclusivity is apparent. Everyone belongs. (2) Service is paramount. Whose feet do we wash? (3) We are no longer stuck in sin and death and legalism, clericalism, sexism, racism and all the other consciousness filters.
2. Why does the Holy Spirit have such a hard time speaking?
3. Why is it so hard to hear the prophets?
4. Why are they still stoned?

5. Why was Jesus crucified?
6. Why are the charisms of the community silenced?
7. What can we really hope from the Holy Spirit?